DESERT
FOOD CHAINS

Bobbie Kalman & Kelley MacAulay
Crabtree Publishing Company
www.crabtreebooks.com

Created by Bobbie Kalman

Dedicated by Craig Culliford
For my daughter Amy, with love

Editor-in-Chief
Bobbie Kalman

Writing team
Bobbie Kalman
Kelley MacAulay

Substantive editor
Kathryn Smithyman

Editors
Molly Aloian
Kristina Lundblad
Reagan Miller

Art director
Robert MacGregor

Design
Katherine Kantor

Production coordinator
Katherine Kantor

Photo research
Crystal Foxton

Special thanks to
New England Hiking Holidays

Consultant
Patricia Loesche, Ph.D., Animal Behavior Program,
Department of Psychology, University of Washington

Photographs
Bruce Coleman Inc.: Bob & Clara Calhoun: page 17 (bottom)
James Kamstra: pages 15 (top), 21 (bottom), 25
Photo by Tina Kennedy: page 29
Robert McCaw: pages 14 (top), 20 (bottom), 23 (bottom)
New England Hiking Holidays: page 30
Tom Stack & Associates: Joe McDonald: page 19
Other images by Adobe Image Library, Corbis, Corel, Digital Stock,
Digital Vision, and Photodisc

Illustrations
Barbara Bedell: pages 3 (kangaroo rat, agave, scorpian, and rabbit), 5 (rabbit),
  6-7 (scorpian, kangaroo rat, rabbit, turtle, agave, and mouse), 14, 16, 24 (ground
  and agave), 25 (right), 26 (kangaroo rat, rabbit, and coyote)
Katherine Kantor: pages 3 (rocks), 5 (grass), 6-7 (cactus with flowers andgrass), 9,
  10, 11, 13, 26 (cactus, snake, and grass)
Cori Marvin: page 24 (bat)
Jeannette McNaughton: page 25 (left)
Margaret Amy Reiach: series logo, pages 3 (spider and snail), 5 (coyote and sun),
  6-7 (coyote, snail, and spider), 20, 24 (earthworm)
Bonna Rouse: pages 3 (cactus), 6-7 (cactus and weeds)

Crabtree Publishing Company

www.crabtreebooks.com   1-800-387-7650

Copyright © **2005 CRABTREE PUBLISHING COMPANY.**
All rights reserved. No part of this publication may be
reproduced, stored in a retrieval system or be transmitted in
any form or by any means, electronic, mechanical, photocopying,
recording, or otherwise, without the prior written permission of
Crabtree Publishing Company. In Canada: We acknowledge the
financial support of the Government of Canada through the
Book Publishing Industry Development Program (BPIDP) for
our publishing activities.

Cataloging-in-Publication Data
Kalman, Bobbie.
Desert food chains / Bobbie Kalman & Kelley MacAulay.
    p. cm. -- (The food chains series)
Includes index.
  ISBN 0-7787-1944-8 (RLB) -- ISBN 0-7787-1990-1 (pbk.)
  1. Desert ecology--Juvenile literature. 2. Food chains (Ecology)--Juvenile
literature. I. MacAulay, Kelley. II. Title.
QH541.5.D4K35 2004
577.54--dc22
                                                                2004013375
                                                                LC

**Published in
the United States**
PMB 16A
350 Fifth Ave.
Suite 3308
New York, NY
10118

**Published
in Canada**
616 Welland Ave.
St. Catharines, Ontario
L2M 5V6

**Published in the
United Kingdom**
White Cross Mills
Hight Town, Lancaster
LA1 4XS

**Published
in Australia**
386 Mt. Alexander Rd.
Ascot Vale (Melbourne)
VIC 3032

Contents

What is a food chain?

The Earth is full of living things. Some living things are animals, and others are plants. Most animals and plants need the same things to stay alive. They need air, water, sunlight, and food.

Nutrients from food

Food provides plants and animals with **nutrients**, or the substances they need to grow and to stay healthy. Food also provides animals with **energy**, or power. Animals use energy to breathe air, to grow, and to move around.

This desert iguana is getting nutrients and energy from a cactus plant.

A food chain

All animals eat other living things to get energy. Some animals eat plants. Others eat animals that feed on plants. For example, rabbits eat grass, and coyotes eat rabbits. This pattern of eating and being eaten is called a **food chain**. Every plant and animal belongs to at least one food chain.

Energy for plants

Plants do not get food in the same way as animals do. Do you know how plants get food? They **produce**, or make, it using the sun's energy! To see how a food chain works, look at the diagram on the right.

Energy from the sun

Green plants trap some of the sun's energy and use it to make their own food. They use some of the energy as food and store the rest.

sun

grass

When an animal such as a jackrabbit eats a plant, it gets some of the energy that was stored in the plant. The jackrabbit gets less of the sun's energy than the grass received.

jackrabbit

When a coyote eats a jackrabbit, energy is passed to the coyote through the jackrabbit. The coyote gets less of the sun's energy than the amount the jackrabbit received.

coyote

5

An energy pyramid

As animals eat food, energy is passed from one living thing to another. The **energy pyramid** on the right shows this flow of energy. The pyramid is wide at the first level to show that there are many plants that make food energy. At the second level, there are fewer living things, and the pyramid narrows to show it. The pyramid is even narrower at the top. Why is that?

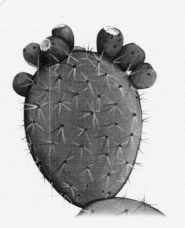

Third level: carnivores

The third level of a food chain is made up of **carnivores**. Carnivores are animals that get food energy by eating other animals. Carnivores are the **secondary consumers** in a food chain. Secondary consumers eat primary consumers. They are at the top of the food chain, where there is much less energy. As a result, there are fewer carnivores than there are herbivores or plants. The pyramid is narrowest at this level to show the fewest living things.

Second level: herbivores

The second level of a food chain is made up of **herbivores**. Herbivores are animals that eat mainly plants. Herbivores are the **primary consumers** in a food chain. A primary consumer is the first living thing in a food chain that must eat to get energy. Herbivores must eat many plants to get the energy they need to survive. For this reason, there are fewer herbivores than there are plants.

First level: plants

The **primary**, or first, level of a food chain is made up of plants. Plants are called **primary producers** because they make food and are the first level in a food chain. There are more plants than there are animals. It takes many plants to feed all the animals in a food chain!

The Sonoran Desert

Cold deserts, such as the Arctic, do not receive much snow each year. The snow is often deep because it does not melt.

This book is about food chains in the Sonoran Desert. A desert is a natural area that receives less than ten inches (25 cm) of rain or snow each year. Very little rain or snow makes deserts dry places. Most deserts are hot, but some are cold! Cold deserts receive snow. Hot deserts receive rain. Like most deserts, the Sonoran is a hot desert.

Some hot deserts are huge sandy areas where few living things are able to grow.

Sudden changes

The Sonoran Desert is in the southern parts of Arizona and California. It stretches into northern Mexico, as well. The Sonoran Desert is a place where the weather changes quickly. It is very hot during the day but is often freezing cold at night! The weather is dry for long periods of time. After a dry period, there may be heavy rains that cover the land with water.

The United States

Mexico

The Sonoran Desert has two rainy seasons. The rain helps many living things survive.

Food for desert plants

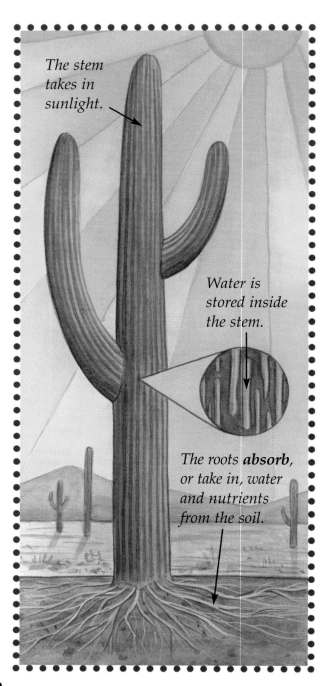

The stem takes in sunlight.

Water is stored inside the stem.

The roots absorb, or take in, water and nutrients from the soil.

Green plants are the only living things that make their own food using the sun's energy. Making food from sunlight is called **photosynthesis**.

Photosynthesis

Plants contain a green **pigment**, or color, called **chlorophyll**. Chlorophyll catches sunlight. To make food, chlorophyll combines sunlight with water from the soil and **carbon dioxide**, a gas found in air. The food plants make is **glucose**, a type of sugar. Plants use some of the food they make and store the rest.

Chlorophyll is found in the leaves of most green plants, but many desert plants do not have leaves. In desert plants, such as the saguaro cactus shown left, photosynthesis takes place mainly in the stems.

Working at night

All green plants absorb carbon dioxide through tiny holes called **stomata**. Most plants absorb this gas during the day. As plants open their stomata, some water comes out of these holes. Water **evaporates**, or turns into water vapor, quickly in the hot desert sun. Desert plants cannot afford to lose any water! To prevent water loss, many desert plants open their stomata only at night.

Plants are good for the air

During photosynthesis, green plants make large amounts of **oxygen**. Animals need oxygen to survive. Photosynthesis helps animals by making oxygen. Photosynthesis also helps them by using up carbon dioxide. Too much carbon dioxide in the air can harm animals.

At night, the open stomata take in carbon dioxide and release oxygen.

11

Sonoran Desert plants

The Sonoran Desert is a difficult place for plants to grow. It is hot and dry. For most of the year, the soil is thin and sandy. It has few of the nutrients plants need to survive.

A few **species**, or types, of plants have **adapted**, or changed, to be able to survive in the desert. These pages show some of the ways desert plants are suited to their harsh home.

The saguaro cactus

The saguaro cactus grows only in the Sonoran Desert. The stem of the saguaro has **pleats**, or folds. The pleats **expand**, or grow bigger, to store water during the rainy seasons. Like most cacti, the saguaro has a thick, waxy skin covered with **spines**. The spines keep animals from eating the cacti. The waxy coating helps stop the cacti from losing water.

The saguaro cactus can grow up to 56 feet (17 m) tall. It usually lives over 200 years!

A short life

Some desert plants avoid the hottest months of the year by staying alive only for short periods of time. Many of the desert's spring flowers live only for a few weeks. They flower during the spring rainy season and scatter new seeds before they die. The seeds remain **dormant** until the next rainy season. Dormant seeds do not grow until there is enough moisture for them to survive.

Plants lose water through their leaves, so most desert plants have very small leaves or no leaves at all.

Finding water

Cacti and shrubs are the most common desert plants. Desert plants do not grow close together. They need room to spread out their long **shallow** roots. Shallow roots grow sideways instead of growing down into the ground.

The roots are long so plants can get water from a large area of land. They are shallow so that they can absorb water before the water sinks deep into the ground. The plants store the water in their stems and leaves. Plants that store water are called **succulents**.

13

Desert herbivores

The desert cottontail rabbit is a grazer. It eats mainly grass.

There are more species of plants and animals living in the Sonoran Desert than in any other desert in the world! Some Sonoran Desert animals are herbivores. Desert herbivores have to eat many plants to get the food energy they need.

Types of plant-eaters

Not all herbivores eat the same plants. Herbivores that eat grass and small plants near the ground are called **grazers**. Those that eat the leaves, shoots, and twigs of plants are known as **browsers**.

The desert bighorn sheep is a browser. It eats mainly leaves and twigs.

Different foods

Herbivores eat different parts of plants. When desert flowers are in bloom, butterflies, bees, and many birds feed on **nectar**. Nectar is a sweet liquid found in flowers. Many small animals and some birds eat the seeds, roots, and fruits of desert plants.

Collared peccaries eat many parts of cactus plants. They also feed on different plant roots. The roots supply the water and nutrients these animals need to survive.

The desert tortoise eats the red fruits that grow on the prickly pear cactus.

15

Sonoran Desert animals

Desert animals must work hard to find food, water, and shelter from the heat. Some animals have special body parts that help them survive. The desert tortoise, shown right, stores water in its body. After drinking a large amount of water, it does not need to drink again for years! These pages show some of the other ways animals survive in the Sonoran Desert.

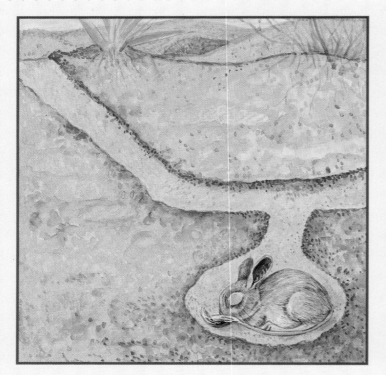

A deep sleep

During the hottest time of the year, some desert animals, such as this gerboa, go into a deep sleep called **estivation**. Animals that estivate stay asleep for weeks at a time! While they are sleeping, the bodies of the animals use very little energy. The animals do not need to eat or drink water.

*Animals estivate in **burrows**, or underground tunnels, that they have dug as shelters.*

The night life

On a hot summer day, it can seem as if no animals live in the Sonoran Desert! To avoid the heat, most desert animals, such as these kit foxes, are **nocturnal**. Nocturnal animals come out at **dusk**, or in the evening, and hunt during the night. They spend their days sleeping in cool underground burrows or in shady places.

The little pocket mouse spends most of its life underground. The mouse has small pouches in its mouth that can hold many seeds. It uses the pockets to gather enough food so it can stay in its burrow for months! When the food runs out, the mouse leaves its burrow to gather more seeds. It then returns underground.

17

Desert carnivores

One animal, two meals

Some carnivores eat both herbivores and other carnivores. For example, a bobcat, shown above, is a secondary consumer when it eats a squirrel, which is a herbivore. When it eats a roadrunner, which is a carnivore, the bobcat is a tertiary consumer.

Many desert animals are carnivores that get food energy by eating other animals. Most carnivores are **predators**. Predators are animals that hunt and kill other animals for food. The animals that predators eat are called **prey**. Many predators are secondary consumers because they eat herbivores, but some also eat carnivores. When carnivores eat other carnivores, they are called **tertiary consumers**.

*The horned lizard feeds mainly on harvester ants. Animals that feed on insects are called **insectivores**.*

18

Important animals

Predators are very important animals in a food chain. Without predators, there would be too many herbivores, and soon all the plants would be eaten.

Healthy food chains

Carnivores are also important because they help keep desert animal **populations** healthy.

Carnivores usually feed on prey that are helpless, such as animals that are very young, sick, or old. Carnivores **prey on**, or hunt, weak animals because they are the easiest to catch. By hunting weak animals, carnivores remove them from a food chain. Without the weak animals, there is more food for the healthy animals.

*Harris' hawks are carnivores that live in the Sonoran Desert. They prey on many small animals, including rabbits, **rodents**, snakes, and lizards.*

Hunters and scavengers

Carnivores have many ways of catching food. Some predators, such as desert tarantulas, catch prey by **ambushing**, or quickly attacking prey from a hiding spot. Mountain lions and some other predators sneak up on their prey and then chase it. Most predators also have special body parts that help them catch their prey. For example, many desert spiders, snakes, and scorpions inject **venom**, or poison, into prey.

The Gambel's quail uses its long toes to dig up insects that live underground.

Feeding on carrion

Some carnivores are **scavengers**. Scavengers are animals that feed mainly on **carrion**, or dead animals. Black vultures, such as the one shown right, are Sonoran Desert scavengers. They wait until an animal has finished eating its prey and then feed on whatever is left.

Cleaning the desert

Scavengers help keep the Sonoran Desert clean. They also use the leftover food energy from the bodies of dead animals, which would otherwise go to waste.

The caracara is an eagle that feeds mainly on dead animals. Caracaras even follow vultures to food and attack the vultures until they leave their meal.

21

Desert omnivores

It can be hard for animals to find food in the desert, so most desert animals are **omnivores**. Omnivores eat both plants and other animals. They are **opportunistic feeders**. Opportunistic feeders eat any food that is available.

Omnivores do not have much difficulty finding food because they eat almost anything! Coyotes, such as the one above, are omnivores. They eat rabbits, mice, squirrels, insects, and lizards. They also eat fruits and other plant parts.

Changing foods

An omnivore's **diet**, or the types of foods it eats, often changes with the seasons. Many desert-bird omnivores eat insects for part of the year and plant foods during other periods. For example, the roadrunner, shown below, eats mainly insects and small reptiles in the summer. In winter, when prey is harder to find, the roadrunner eats plant foods.

The collared lizard runs from rock to rock chasing and eating insects. It also eats desert fruits.

Desert decomposers

Scavengers are not the only living things that help keep the desert clean. **Decomposers** help, too! Decomposers are living things that eat dead plants and animals to get the last bits of stored food energy. **Bacteria**, worms, termites, and snails are common decomposers found in the Sonoran Desert. Decomposers make up **detritus food chains**, such as the one shown right. Detritus is material that is **decomposing**, or breaking down.

A detritus food chain

When a plant or an animal, such as this bat, dies, it becomes dead material in the soil.

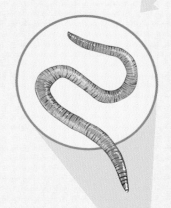

Decomposers in the soil, such as this worm, eat the dead material and get some of the energy stored in it. The decomposers then pass some of this energy into the soil through their droppings.

The droppings of decomposers add nutrients to the soil. The nutrients help new plants grow.

Note: The arrows point toward the things that receive energy.

Leftover nutrients

Decomposers help keep the soil healthy. They release the leftover energy that is trapped in dead material back into the soil. The leftover energy contains nutrients that new plants get from the soil. Without these nutrients, plants could not grow, and all other living things would soon starve.

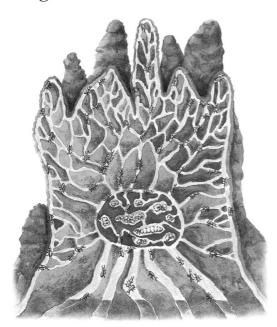

Termites are important decomposers in the Sonoran Desert. Without termites, the soil would be filled with dead material.

It can take millipedes hundreds of years to break down large plants or trees, such as this dead saguaro cactus.

A desert food web

Most living things belong to more than one food chain. There are many food chains in the Sonoran Desert. A single food chain includes a plant, a herbivore, and a carnivore. When an animal from one food chain eats a plant or an animal that belongs to a different food chain, two food chains connect. Two or more connecting food chains make a **food web**. Most food webs include many kinds of plants and animals.

A summer food web

This diagram shows a summer food web in the Sonoran Desert. The arrows point toward the living things that receive food energy.

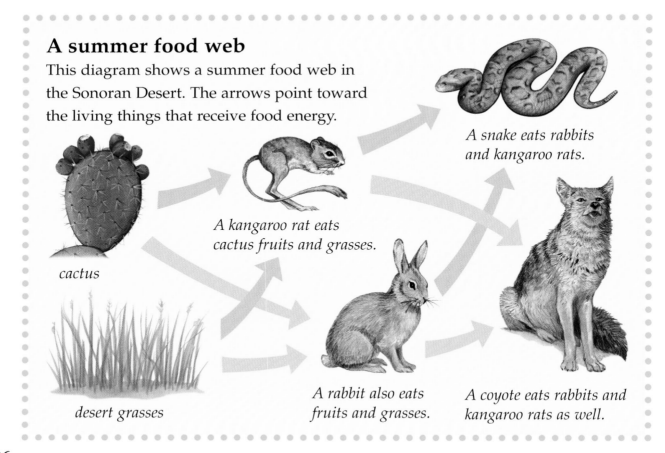

A snake eats rabbits and kangaroo rats.

A kangaroo rat eats cactus fruits and grasses.

cactus

A rabbit also eats fruits and grasses.

A coyote eats rabbits and kangaroo rats as well.

desert grasses

Changing food webs

Food chains in the Sonoran Desert change with the seasons. Many desert plants grow during certain seasons. They are part of a food web only when they are alive. Many desert animals estivate. When an animal is estivating, it is not a part of a food web because estivating animals do not eat.

Some animals sleep during the summer, whereas others sleep during the winter months. The gila monster, shown above, estivates during winter. It is part of a food web only when it is active during the summer months.

During the winter months, gopher snakes sleep under rocks or in burrows.

27

Dangers to desert food webs

The Sonoran Desert is a special area. Some Sonoran Desert plants and animals do not live anywhere else in the world! People threaten the Sonoran Desert in many ways, however. When large numbers of people move into the desert, they take up a lot of space to build cities, farms, and recreational areas. When people need space, they **clear**, or remove the plants from, large areas of desert land. Some of the animals that live in these spaces must move to other areas to find food. Many desert animals, however, die when their space is taken over.

Hungry carnivores

Clearing large areas of desert causes many problems. When plants are removed, many herbivores die from a lack of food. When the herbivores die, carnivores, such as the mountain lion shown left, do not have enough to eat. They sometimes go to cities in search of food and may eat pet dogs or cats that are outdoors. Many people are afraid of these large carnivores, so they shoot and kill them.

Clearing the land

Hundreds of miles of desert land have been cleared so crops could be planted and so cows and other animals have space to graze. Grazing animals eat many of the plants that desert animals need for food. Both farm animals and crops need large amounts of water, which must be pumped by machines into the desert from rivers that are far away. Pumping water from rivers can cause rivers to dry up forever.

Special soil

Many people enjoy visiting the Sonoran Desert. When too many people walk on desert soil, however, desert plants suffer. Desert soil is covered by a special crust that keeps nutrients in the soil. When people walk, drive, or ride bicycles over the soil, they destroy the crust. Grazing animals also ruin the soil's crust. When the crust is damaged, desert plants lose the important nutrients that they need to survive.

Large areas of land where many desert animals and plants live are often destroyed to make golf courses. Keeping golf courses green also requires a lot of water.

29

Helping the desert

There are many people trying to save the Sonoran Desert. You can help save the desert, too! One of the best ways to help is by learning all you can about the Sonoran Desert. You can learn about this special desert from this book, other library books, and on the Internet. Share the information you learn with your family and friends. These pages show some of the ways people are helping the Sonoran Desert.

National parks

National parks are natural areas protected by the government. They give plants and animals safe places to live. Many national parks have been created in the Sonoran Desert. People can visit the parks, but they must stay on **trails**, or paths. By staying on trails, people do not disturb the animals and plants, or destroy the desert soil's special crust. People can keep the parks clean by throwing their garbage in trash cans. Visitors can help national parks by following the rules.

Studying the desert

Scientists study the Sonoran Desert and the plants and animals that live there. Studying the desert helps scientists find out how the desert is damaged. The scientists and other groups of people can then work to pass laws that will protect the Sonoran Desert. For example, it is now **illegal**, or against the law, for farmers to graze **livestock** in many areas of the Sonoran Desert. This law protects the natural homes of many desert animals, including the bobcat shown above.

Some cities in the Sonoran Desert are helping local birds by asking people to grow desert plants around homes and other buildings. The plants give many types of birds places to live in the cities.

Glossary

Note: Boldfaced words that are defined in the text may not appear in the glossary.

bacteria Tiny single-celled living things

carbon dioxide A gas found in the air that is needed by plants to make food

dormant Describing a state during which seeds do not grow because there is not enough water or sunlight

energy The power living things get from food that helps them move, grow, and stay healthy

estivate To sleep for long periods of time

livestock Animals raised by people for food

oxygen A colorless, odorless gas in the air that animals need to breathe

pigment A natural color found in plants and animals

population The total number of a type of plant or animal living in a certain place

rodents A group of animals that have small bodies and front teeth, which never stop growing

spines Sharp needles that stick out of cactus plants

Index

2 3 4 5 6 7 8 9 0 Printed in the U.S.A. 4 3 2 1 0 9 8 7 6